Deer Hunting Handbook for Beginners:

Detailed Guide on How to Effectively Hunt Deer & Get the Best Catches Using Amazing Shots & Secrets; Mistakes to Avoid & the Tools Needed & So On

By

Markus J. Muench

Copyright@2020

TABLE OF CONTENTS

CHAPTER ONE

INTRODUCTION

The chasing of different types of wild deer has been a national energy and custom for innumerable ages. Numerous Native American stories and records are filled with the chasing and collecting of whitetails. Numerous early pilgrims of the West saw whitetail and donkey deer as a plentiful, important food hotspot for themselves and their families. Shockingly, the twentieth century saw a sharp decrease in the collecting of deer due to overhunting and a diminishing populace of whitetail all through the United States. Be that as it may, because of the industrious endeavours of state protection divisions and capable trackers, numerous states currently brag near at least 200,000 reaped deer every year. Truth be told, in numerous states deer are overpopulated and are compromising woodland development and cultivates and may likewise build the danger of lyme infection in people in territories where their numbers are especially high. Mindful trackers assume a significant job in overseeing deer populaces so the groups don't pressure biological systems.

Your may have ended up considering deer chasing at once or another however never truly realized where to begin. The upsides of deer chasing are as follows:

-New, natural, lean meat

-Time spent in nature

-Developed endurance/outdoorsman aptitudes

-Self-improvement as a man/supplier

-Character improvement

-Marksmanship

-Convention

With this introduction on deer chasing, and some training and coaching from experienced trackers, you ought to have the option to run away and hide with trust in quest for your first in a long and upbeat arrangement of deer. The next chapters reveal the a to z of DEER HUNNTING THAT you need to know!

CHAPTER TWO

THE NECESSITIES OF DEER HUNTING

In this way, you've been considering getting into deer chasing. Possibly this is on the grounds that you're keen on gathering your own meat or perhaps this is on the grounds that you consider it to be an approach to put your shooting abilities to pragmatic use. In any case, deer chasing can be an entirely agreeable and profitable approach to invest your energy. With Tennessee deer season and RECOIL's Hunter Games both right around the bend, I've had deer on the mind practically relentless, so this was the ideal event to discuss how to begin deer chasing.

Getting Legal

The primary thing to take care of is getting your hands on a duplicate of your state's chasing laws. Contingent upon where you live and whether you are chasing on open or private terrains, the guidelines will differ as will the sort of permit you should chase legitimately. Furthermore, your state may require various kinds of licenses dependent on your weapon of decision, so it's useful to settle on this choice from the get-go.

Equipping

Rigging choice is one territory where individuals have a wide range of feelings or tastes. The guidance beneath is my position on apparatus, and it's surely by all account not the only position out there. My way to deal with gear is to keep it insignificant yet high-calibre. I don't care to convey a great deal of poop, so relying upon how far I need to walk or how long I intend to chase, in some cases you won't get me with a knapsack. We should separate this:

Attire

Explicit decisions rely upon the atmosphere where you will chase. The early season where I live is boiling hot and damp, so I wear the lightest weight attire I can discover. I would suggest wearing a lightweight long-sleeved shirt. In the event that chasing from a tree stand or the ground I wear camo, if chasing from a ground dazzle I wear a dark long-sleeved shirt. I quite often apply only a little paint to my face to separate that outline too. For summer, a lightweight boot is extraordinary. I like a lightweight rain boot, as it rains a great deal in the South in the hotter months.

In the colder months, layering is my go-to, with more accentuation set on my feet, hands, and face. Nothing makes it harder to go for the long stretches in a tree remain in winter than having fingers and toes so cool that they hurt. Moreover, this can influence your capacity not exclusively to work your bow or rifles adequately yet in addition makes getting into and out of your tree stand more troublesome. Having a durable, protected, waterproof boot is basic exposed months. Keeping your feet dry ought to consistently be a need.

Game cameras are an incredible method to check whether deer are traveling through a region during shooting hours or around evening time.

Weapon

Landscape and capacity are the two most significant variables while picking a weapon to chase with (outside of the law obviously). In the case of chasing with a bow, rifle, shotgun, or muzzleloader you should know both the constraints of your weapon and yourself, as to separate and the trouble of the shots. On the off chance that you have not worked on shooting past 30 yards with your bow or don't have your bow located in for anything past that separation, try not to be going after a creature. This is valid and comparative with any weapon you decide to utilize. Set aside the effort to guarantee that your weapon is located in or focused and that you know any important leftovers you may require on your chase.

Other Gear

Coming up next is a short rundown of other rigging I generally take with me when I go chasing:

-Wellbeing bridle if chasing from a tree stand

-Stool if chasing from a visually impaired

-Light source (either a headlamp or an electric lamp)

-Blade (one that incorporates a gut snare)

-Thermacell (an incredible speculation in the event that you live some place with loads of mosquitos)

-Rangefinder

Optics

Any supplemental apparatus that you have to shoot your weapon (ammunition, mags, wrist discharge for bow, and so forth.)

While picking a spot to chase, search for signs that deer have been in the territory.

CHAPTER THREE

PICK YOUR WEAPON, AND VITAL TIPS

Vintage trackers in woods talking rifles inclining toward trees.

The primary spot to begin with deer chasing is to choose your technique. Would you like to be a rifle tracker or would you like to be an elective strategies tracker (bow, atlatl, gun, and so on.)? A significant number of us started as rifle trackers since it is the most open spot to begin.

Since this is an apprentice's introduction on deer chasing, we would suggest beginning with a rifle and afterward stretching out as your inclinations direct.

While picking a deer rifle, one must consider spending plan and fit. At the point when I as of late addressed Ken Jorgensen at Ruger Firearms he suggested that a tracker finds a rifle that:

Finishes the undertaking successfully (for this situation, murder a deer rapidly)

-Fits the shooter

-Can be shot well

It merits your time and endeavors to go to a firearm store and "test" possible rifles. Get the firearms, shoulder them, control the activities, sight-in an item on the floor or roof, and simply perceive how you like them. A couple of models of firearms to investigate as a spending plan amicable beginning stage may be:

-Winchester Model 70

-Savage Trophy Hunter XP

-Weatherby Vanguard

-Remington Model 700

-Ruger American Rifle

To finish the errand adequately in deer chasing requires a cartridge with a little punch. In any case, in the event that you are new to firearm bores, picking the best bore for yourself resembles picking some irregular battery off the rack and trusting that it will work in your TV distant. You need the best possible measure of intensity joined with your capacity to oversee pull back. A couple of regular gauges for deer chasing are as per the following:

.270 Winchester

.308 Winchester

.30-30 Winchester

.30-06 Springfield

7mm Remington Magnum

These bores are top choices among deer trackers and outdoorsmen. On the off chance that you can, attempt to shoot these bores before you get one to see which you like; every cartridge nearly appears to have its own character. On the off chance that you can't fire before focusing on a rifle, read and watch whatever number surveys as could reasonably be expected to instruct yourself on their employments. In the event that you pick a sufficient gauge and the weapon fits you well, you have won 2/3 of the fight. All you need to do currently is practice.

An incredible spot to begin when rehearsing is to shoot from a seat towards a fixed objective, set at 25 yards. You need to deal with setting bunches on the objective that are on the whole striking close to a similar position. At that point, as you get more acquainted with the firearm, move your objective out to 100 yards and work on something very similar. A 100-yard shot is a decent spot to start as a first-time tracker. As you get more acquainted with the firearm, you will have the option to work out to farther shot arrangements. Be that as it may, for your initial, 100 yards is a decent separation.

Tracker's Safety Course

When you have gained the weapon and abilities required to chase effectively, there is one last advance of the procedure: getting confirmed and authorized by your state protection division. Guidelines on turning out to be authorized shift from state to state. Most states require any individual who wishes to legitimately chase with a gun to take a tracker's wellbeing course. The necessities of the course, including the age at which one must be authorized, fluctuates from state to state. The best hotspot for this data would be your state protection office site or a close by preservation office.

Most tracker wellbeing courses incorporate a 4-hour course and a composed test. You can read for the test on the web or with a guidance booklet gave by your protection division. At that point, when you have arranged for the class, basically register for your 4-hour affirmation course on the web or face to face. The vast majority of these classes are for nothing out of pocket. When you have breezed through your assessment and gotten accreditation, you are currently ready to buy your grants for your chase.

In the event that you don't know yet on the off chance that deer chasing is for you, you may investigate a transient choice to obtain your tracker grants. In numerous states, there are tracker disciple programs that permit you to take to the field nearby another ensured tracker that has finished their tracker's security course. This permits you to purchase allows and chase as such for a short time before you take a tracker's security course for yourself. That way, you can choose if it is a solid match for you.

Prior to taking to the field, it is imperative to peruse your state's chasing guidelines altogether every single year that you chase. These guidelines, because of the board needs, can change yearly.

Dressing for the Field

The subsequent stage is to equip yourself with chasing gear. This is the place a tracker can truly lose themselves in the inundation of fragrances, camos, and different items that apparently offer boundless achievement. Here are the stripped down necessities when you head into the forested areas on your chase:

-Your weapon

-Burst orange cap and vest (wear this 100% of the time – it can spare your life)

-A crate of ammo (except if you shoot and miss a great deal, this should get the job done)

-A decent, sharp blade (for field dressing your deer)

-Tall elastic gloves (for field dressing your deer)

-A spotlight (for following your deer)

-Warm gloves, cap, and coat (for those cool November chases)

-Your grants (the most fundamental thing)

-A ziplock pack, zip tie, and a pen (contingent upon your state laws for labeling your game)

-Finding a Place to Hunt

Vintage delineation trackers in kayak deer in vessel

When you have secured the entirety of your fundamentals and are currently a capable marksman, the following stage is finding a spot to chase. In the event that you are a landowner with enough land to chase, you are in karma. If not, you have to either locate some open chasing land in your general vicinity or become companions with a portion of your nearby ranchers and landowners. Never chase some place that you have not acquired authorization to chase. Assemble a decent connection with those sufficiently caring to allow you to chase and, in the event that you are honored with a gather, share a part of it with your host.

At the point when you discover land, either pick an area in a lush region that considers deer and different creatures to cruise by, or decide to chase the edge of an open field. This is the place pre-season exploring turns out to be significant. When chasing just because, we suggest chasing from ground level, yet on the off chance that you incline toward a stand, ensure you pick one that is steady and simple to move into with a rifle and your rigging. These kinds of stands are called tripod stands and can be found at your neighborhood open air stores. These stands increment the expense of your chase significantly, so choose whether a stand is fundamental before making the speculation. The favorable position to chasing out of a stand is that you are not eye level with the deer so it is more diligently for them to see you.

You need to ensure that your stand or ground area is along a way that deer travel much of the time. Something else that you ought to consider when picking your stand or chasing spot is your solace level. In the event that you can't reliably make long shots, an open field isn't the spot for you. You should take a stab at setting up in certain hardwoods where the main shot that you can take is a nearby one. Ensure you show up to your chasing area before dawn or a couple of hours before nightfall, in order to limit your quality. At that point, calmly trust that your game will show up.

One approach to expand the chances in support of yourself is to put out a salt lick, a food plot, or different attractants close to your chasing spot before the season opens. These pull in deer, just as other untamed life, and make your chasing area part of their standard daily schedule. One interesting point while doing this, be that as it may, is the expected necessity to end your attractants before the season (typically 10 days earlier). Else, you might be managing a goading infringement and a colossal fine. In the event that you make this stride, know about the entirety of the duties in question and play it safe to guarantee a moral, lawful chase. Each state is unique, so check your state's laws about food plots and bedeviling. When attempting to choose what might work best for you, thoroughly consider your chasing circumstance and responsibility level. It requires some investment, land, and control to plant and keep up a plot. Ensure that you are prepared to make that responsibility of both time and assets.

Making the Effort

When making an effort, you generally need to trust that a deer will stand broadside, which implies that they are standing opposite to your rifle barrel. At the point when you can see from nose to tail, bring your sights onto the deer simply behind the front shoulder, as you need to hit the lungs as well as heart. Unobtrusively take the weapon off security, take a major breath and let it out, and equally press the trigger until the firearm discharge. Quickly, rack the jolt and chamber a live shell.

In the event that you have hit your imprint, watch where the deer takes off. Stand by anyplace somewhere in the range of 15 and 30 minutes before following and seeking after. This will give the deer a lot of time to rests and terminate. In the event that you attempt to pursue the deer when it is shot, you are going to put unneeded weight on the creature. This will likewise make more adrenaline be created by the deer, which will make it travel farther. The extra flood of hormones and synthetic substances can possibly bring about your venison building up a solid "gamey" or unwanted flavor. In the event that the deer has crossed a property line, ensure that you have authorization to be on that property before seeking after. It is as yet considered intruding on the off chance that you are pursuing an injured creature. Ensure you realize who claims the entirety of the land around you and how to connect with them. It's your duty to bend over backward to recoup any deer you shoot.

CHAPTER FOUR

LOCATING THE DEER, SLAUGHTERING AND WHAT TO DO AFTER KILLING

Finding, however making sense of the development examples of the deer where you will chase is indispensable to a fruitful season— yet it tends to be dubious. Because the deer are frequenting a territory in summer doesn't mean they will do likewise in fall or winter. There are numerous variables to consider when exploring for deer, and instead of attempt to spread them over here, I'm getting that activity out to QDMA. The Quality Deer Management Association utilizes exploration to instruct trackers pretty much all parts of whitetail science with an end goal to create better deer and better trackers. This article works admirably of spreading out techniques for finding a zone to chase deer. Moreover, QDMA is an amazing wellspring of data for everything identified with deer chasing.

In the event that chasing from a ground dazzle, set aside some additional effort to brush it in, with the goal that it mixes into the earth however much as could reasonably be expected. Would you be able to recognize the ground daze in this image?

Slaughtering a Deer

We should discuss shot arrangement. Helpless shot situation expands the odds that you will

wound and not kill the deer or end up on an
hours-in length following journey that might
possibly end in progress. I'm not very pleased to
concede that I know this as a matter of fact and
trust me it's a disappointment you need to
maintain a strategic distance from. Knowing the
life structures of a deer is the pivotal factor in
realizing where to put your shot.

Aroma Control

Deer have a sharp feeling of smell, so covering
your human aroma is the greatest hindrance to
drawing near to deer. There are different items
intended to help spread your fragrance, for
example, body cleanser, cleanser, clothing
cleanser, and showers that you can apply for
additional spread while in the field. I suggest
utilizing these, however that isn't ordinarily
enough. Probably the most ideal approaches to
shield deer from finding your trail is to ensure
that the bearing of the breeze isn't making it
blow your fragrance towards the deer. There
have been commonly when, notwithstanding
bending over backward to cover my aroma, deer

have gotten downwind of me and afterward continued to tell the entirety of their companions I was there. Chase over.

After The Kill

Congrats on an effective deer chase! In the event that you are handling your own deer, presently is the point at which the work truly begins. This video subtleties a successful, brisk, and basic strategy for cleaning and handling deer. Note that not all states will expect you to expel the top of the deer, so you ought to acquaint yourself with the relevant laws in your state.

In the event that you don't feel good handling your own deer, or in case you're similar to me and are simply excessively sluggish, taking it to a meat processor is an extraordinary choice. Frequently meat processors can give you alternatives with regards to what cuts of meat you might want, and as far as I can tell, they improve work handling the meat since well, that is their activity.

On the off chance that for reasons unknown you would prefer not to keep the meat from your deer chase, kindly don't junk it. Associations like Hunters For The Hungry have been set up to lessen the misuse of wild game while additionally accommodating those out of luck. You can find out the nearest HFH section in your general vicinity.

Let's Dine

Since you have the entirety of this delightful meat, what do you do with it? As far as I can tell, individuals assume that venison must be cooked in some extremely unique manner to taste great, and this isn't accurate. I would state if there is

one thing to think about cooking venison, it's that it is lean so you should take care not to overcook it and I generally add somewhat fat to my venison regardless of how I cook it. To keep it basic, any way that I would utilize hamburger in a formula or dish, I use venison: ground meat for tacos or bolognese sauce, burgers, steaks, or meals, and so forth.

CHAPTER FIVE

INSTRUCTIONS YOU SHOULD TAKE TO GET STARTED AS A NEW HUNTER, AND APPROACHES TO MASTER HUNTING

Make sense of What you'd prefer to do

At the point when you state, you'd prefer to chase, that is a lot of like stating you'd prefer to play sports. The sorts of chasing you can appreciate in the United States is dissimilar to anyplace else on the planet. You can discreetly descend a stream tuning in for spring turkeys, stand firm along edge tops for a wily buck or wander the high nation at the tallness of the elk trench. Set aside some effort to settle on what sort of chasing you'd prefer to appreciate and afterward set a course to do it!

Possess Safety Card for Hunters Plus Making Acquaintances with Persons in this Field

This is a significant piece of your chasing training since it'll show you how to lead a legitimate and moral chase. Countless persons who have never though it do not comprehend that there are seasons as well as restrictions on when plus where you can do chasing and what is permitted when. The game laws can get

befuddling so study and take notes at your
course.

The tracker's wellbeing course is additionally a
fantastic time for you to warm up to individuals
that are either as of now in the chasing society or
will be soon. About each wildlife superintendent,
or Fish and Game representative of your state
wants to chase and these individuals know
where the neighborhood game is in the zone,
and know the land and club proprietor for sure!

Get into the field! (More Explanation)

This may appear to be guaranteed, however such
a large number of individuals ignore this basic
reality, you can't murder them from the sofa,
and when you're an amateur you can't gain from
the kitchen.

An extraordinary spot to go to learn are places
where chasing is restricted yet outdoors and
climbing is. State parks, untamed life shelters,
and mountain biking clubs are generally
awesome approaches to see proof of deer

conduct. Perusing deer signs and picking stand locales is a short-lived ability. Same with calling, shaking or following. Go out and practice all year and you'll show signs of improvement a lot quicker than if you restrict yourself to simply chasing season.

Miracle, Read, Ask Questions and Learn about your New Hobby

There's not a viable alternative for instruction. No, you don't should have the option to compose a doctoral proposal on deer conduct, yet knowing deer science, similar to deer signs and deer chasing strategies, is an awesome asset for figuring out how to chase. Searching for deer sign is simpler when you've seen it before in a book or heard the turkey call you're attempting to mimic. Find out about neighborhood game examples, for example, relocation, favored food sources and each sort of tree in your area.

Purchase the Hunting Gear you need and Practice

It's ideal to pause and purchase your rigging after you realize what you're doing. What you think might be a smart thought in the showroom will appear to be unique after you've hauled it slope and dale and the response to this is to jump on the field and test.

Regularly, the better and more able you are in the field, the less rigging you'll require. Extra, this or additional that is the thing that expands your financial plan and puts a strain on your pack. At the point when you purchase your first arrangement of chasing gear ensure you purchase quality things you can utilize, the possibility of "starter gear" will make your time in the forested areas terrible and makes you less powerful. Simply make a point to get your work done and research the right apparatus. You would prefer not to accomplish something senseless like get a .45 ACP handgun for duck chasing.

Set aside Some effort to Slow Down

For some time, chasing is very fun yet after a couple of seasons once you have set up and subsided into a daily schedule of when you'll have your stands, exploring and when to wrap up your seasons. This routine can slaughter your experience and eagerness.

This is a disgrace, ensure each time you go into the forested areas you appreciate it and love nature you're in. In the event that you extravagant new encounters, set aside the effort to go on new chases for new species or make the side trip over to Africa or North to Alaska and never quit learning and getting a charge out of the outside.

The most effective method to begin as a tracker when your father never showed you as a kid.

Approaches to Learn To Hunt Successfully

At the point when you start your chasing, your encounters will be harsh from the outset since you'll have little thought of what you're doing. There are a couple of ways for you to accelerate your expectation to learn and adapt:

Getting in the Field

There's not a viable alternative for experience and getting into the forested areas searching for the game you're chasing. Be it bear, raccoon or deer everything leaves a sign in the forested areas and you should simply figure out how to understand it. Getting out with a camera can assist you with taking pictures to distinguish later what you've found and a GPS will help you not to get lost, simply recall that frequently you won't have cell inclusion in huge woods and provincial territories. Spots to search for a game is, obviously, the zone you'll be chasing in, however don't disregard open lush parks, state stops and places where chasing is shut. Because you won't chase on that bit of ground doesn't mean there isn't something that can be scholarly by looking around there.

Shadowing others

The quickest method to figure out how to chase is to go with somebody who realizes what they're doing. This shows you tips and deceives and above all shows you what not to do. Numerous individuals will overlook what worked for them path before they overlook what didn't work when they're taking care of an issue and they're bound to give what they saw as inadequate.

Discover individuals who appreciate similar kinds of chasing you're keen on and inquire as to whether you can go with them at some point. Numerous trackers will be glad to oblige and you'll have exercises basically. Ensure you comprehend where you're going and what you'll be doing with the goal that you can design and plan and not ruin their chase.

Examining

An excessive number of trackers neglect this part of figuring out how to chase. Finding out about your quarry be it deer, swines or turkey or predators is something to be thankful for.

Finding out about what sorts of living space, what occurs during the mating season for your game and what sort of nourishments and landscape they like. The response to turning into a more viable tracker is to combine information with experience to turn into a genuine woodsman equipped for taking game anyplace.

Chipping in

Probably the most ideal approaches to meet different trackers and get out into the field and learn is to chip in. About each fish and game office, untamed life backing gathering and even some rustic others conscious sanctuaries have activities where you can chip in. Tidy up ventures, controlled consumes, and natural surroundings the executives' ventures furnish you with encounters in helping untamed life and finding out about game conduct.

Be careful about undertakings made to damn trackers, many "natural life gatherings" run slanderous attacks on gatherings, for example, NSSF and the NRA that go to bat for trackers' privileges and you may wind up in an unstable circumstance.

CHAPTER SIX

SOME HUNTING DOS AND DON'TS FOR YOU

Hunting/Chasing Do's

A couple of tips as well as tricks for fledgling trackers:

Chase Where the Deer are

This is misleadingly straightforward yet entangles a great deal of more current trackers who aren't accustomed to getting out there. In the event that you approach two homesteads, one has a 75-section of land wood part stacked with sign and all the neighbours are immersed with deer or a 15,000-open lot that gets little weight, yet additionally minimal sign, pick the 75-section of land ranch! Go to where the deer are thick when you're beginning and you'll have a simpler time.

Go Slow, and Safe

Wellbeing is the most significant thing in the forested areas. While there aren't a huge amount of mix-ups to be made, there are bunches of chances that can have a deadly outcome in the event that you make an inappropriate move. Leave promptly in the first part of the day, ensure you have an arrangement and be sheltered when you're chasing.

Figure out how to Use What You have

Open air gear is fun; however it's more enjoyable to be in the outside. Try not to get folded over the hub in the event that you don't have the most delightful bow, the best tree stand or you need a lighter pair of servers. Figure out how to utilize what you have and work around the difficulties to be effective.

Have an Exit Strategy

What are you going to do if the snow begins to fall before you leave your stand? What occurs on the off chance that you pack a deer or hoard? What now when your truck doesn't begin when you're in the back 40? Having an alternate course of action and a couple of telephone numbers close by can make all the difference, you don't have to have each crisis arranged out however a little idea can go far previously.

Know your Resources

In each unassuming community, there's a wild game butcher, a hounds man, a taxidermist and a wildlife superintendent. You ought to have the quantity of every one of the four. The butcher and taxidermist are a given yet numerous individuals don't comprehend what they need the wildlife superintendent and a hounds man. At some point, you'll witness a game infringement and it'll make you frantic, and one day you'll wound a deer and need assistance discovering it, these two numbers can make all the difference.

Hunting/Chasing Don'ts

A couple of snappy words from the astute:

Chase for Trophies

At the point when you start, search for develop deer and focus on making some great memories in the forested areas, tusks consistently recoil once you jump on the ground.

Stick round Un-Ethical Hunters

These folks are terrible news and you won't alter their perspective. You can at present spend time with them, simply don't go chasing with them. They WILL get looked sooner or up some other time and hit with an infringement.

Take Un-Safe Shortcuts

Leave the poorly conceived notions for individuals who don't go chasing. Your family merits you back home safe when the chase is finished. Try not to get remiss and begin to release security infringement. Go slow and be sheltered.

Depend on Outfitters or Guides

Going for a completely guided chase is an amazing encounter, particularly for debut animal varieties like moose, elk or sheep. Actually, barely any trackers can bear to do this consistently and you'll be more joyful and be more equipped in the forested areas all alone in the event that you genuinely figure out how to chase.

On the off chance that you didn't get the hang of chasing as a child while following alongside grandpa or your father, don't surrender. All you need is an adoration for the outside a smidgen of coarseness to defeat the expectation to absorb information to be an effective tracker.

Before you head out on your first chase ensure you characterize what achievement is, locate a couple of partners that you can incline toward in the good old days and purchase the correct gear for your chase. First and foremost weapons, stands and transportation will gobble up a ton of your financial plan so recall that the probably the best trackers on the planet utilized basic sticks and slippers to slaughter game.

Most trackers are more than ready to assist a beginner and you can have confidence you'll be acknowledged, regardless of whether you start at 6 or 60.

CHAPTER SEVEN

AMAZING HUNTING/CHASING DEER TIPS FOR DEER HUNTERS

Deer chasing tips

Regardless of whether you're a veteran buck tracker or a novice going to the forested areas just because, the tips underneath can assist you with seeing more achievement this season.

NO. 1

Human scent frightens deer. Shower with an aroma free cleanser before each chasing outing, and make an effort not to pollute your chasing garments while in transit to the field. Keep them fixed in a plastic compartment or sack with leaves, soil and other ground flotsam and jetsam from around your remain until you show up at your chasing area. Doing so will permit your chasing apparel to take on the normally happening fragrances that penetrate your chasing area.

NO. 2

Most trackers believe that doe estrous is the most important thing in the world of huge buck fascination. Despite the fact that estrous is an awesome instrument, it's basically that. Shrewd trackers realize that during the early-season it's critical to exploit a buck's regional impulses. The aroma of an estrous doe during early October just doesn't sound good to a buck, however buck fragrance is consistently worth looking at.

NO. 3

During the pinnacle groove, attempt a drag cloth absorbed doe estrous. Regularly a buck will follow the path right to your stand.

NO. 4

Numerous trackers splash down with smell eliminator soon after getting ready, and preceding the journey into the stand, yet experienced trackers will carry a scent eliminator with them to the tree stand. After the stroll to the stand, apply a smell eliminator to your body, giving unique consideration to your cap and hair.

NO. 5

When the very muzzleloader chasing in wet environment, a bit of electrical tape on top the finish of the very barrel will take away dampness. And you really shoot via the tape when it is a perfect time to collect that very buck.

NO. 6

One of the lethal fragrance systems challenges
the approved value of playing the very breeze.
Locate a long segment of wood, or spread via the
breeze going along its very length (blowing goes
from one finish to the next). At the breezy end,
pour some deer aroma at a few zones, at that
point set up high in a tree stand just on the edge
of the lumber. In case you're set up sufficiently
high, your human scent should stream over the
deer.

NO. 7

Work on setting up and bringing down your tree
remains before the season, and do so low on the
tree. Getting into and out of your spot as
discreetly as conceivable is vital to viewing a
decent buck.

NO. 8

You don't need to claim your own plane, or even
by a carrier ticket, to look at ethereal

photographs of your chasing region, and there are no preferred exploring helps over flying photographs. Simply scan Google Maps for your chasing zone.

NO. 9

Abstain from cutting shooting paths and in any case upsetting your chasing territory during the season. An opportunity to clear shooting paths is during summer. Insightful old bucks can get adapted to the smell of newly cut wood, and start to connect it with human predation.

NO. 10

In the event that some disguise is acceptable, at that point most extreme covering is better. Tree stand blinds help to trick the careful eye of a deer, and give the additional advantage of asylum from brutal breezes.

NO. 11

You have a buck on contiguous land designed, however it doesn't traverse to your chasing zone until in the wake of shooting time is finished. What to do? Have a go at enticing the buck to approach your side with a deer bait or by calling.

NO. 12

Make certain to drench yourself with tick repellent when exploring during summer and late-summer. Tick-borne ailments can close down your chasing season, and you don't need it to be over before it's started!

NO. 13

Try not to disparage the significance of having the option to get to your tree stand undetected, and don't feel that going in under the front of dimness will help. Try to utilize a spring or shade of timberland to cover your entrance.

NO. 14

Wash all chasing garments in a non-scented cleanser each time you're making a beeline for the forested areas. Keep them in a plastic sack until showing up at your chasing region.

NO. 15

Take a stab at making a counterfeit scratch. To begin with, put on careful gloves to forestall human smell sullying. Utilizing a stick, scrape the leaves off of a zone about the size of a hubcap.

NO. 16

During the late season, scout for resumed scratches in profound spread. Enduring bucks are hesitant to get in the open nation, yet search for the last hot does in spread.

NO. 17

When there's snow on the ground, search for leaves tossed over a zone where deer have pawed for pole. On the off chance that there's still some pole around, that may be a decent spot to set up and sit tight for the deer's arrival.

NO. 18

You've made the effort, presently what? On the off chance that you discover earthy colored hair and pink or red blood with rises in it, no doubt you got a heart or lung hit. Earthy colored hair and thick, dim red blood shows a hit excessively far back, potentially a liver shot. White hair and watery blood with stomach matter demonstrate an awful hit.

NO. 19

Most tumbles from the tree stand occur while moving into or out of the stand. That is the reason it's essential to consistently wear a full-body security saddle when chasing from a tree stand.

CHAPTER EIGHT

CONCLUSION

When going out in the forested areas looking for deer it is significant that you keep up a high moral norm of conduct. Probably the most ideal approaches to do this is to rehearse with your weapon of decision. The more certain you are with your weapon, the more sympathetic you will be to the deer.

Approach all the land with deference. Anything you pack in, ensure you pack it out. Sadly, there are trackers out there that are not keen on tidying up after themselves. On the off chance that you happen upon refuse (shell housings, food coverings, disposed of fragrances, and so forth.), pack out that junk too, despite the fact that it isn't your own. The more we as a whole work to deal with our regular assets, the more it will be there to appreciate. Ensure that security is consistently at the front line of your reasoning when chasing, regardless of whether you are chasing alone. Mishaps can happen when you are without anyone else, so consistently be excessively careful and guarantee that security rules are being followed.

In conclusion, don't permit yourself to get excessively made up for lost time in the specialized parts of the chase that you neglect to appreciate the experience. Deer chasing is a fun, testing, energizing, and character-assembling route for you to take care of your family while keeping up a convention that ranges a long ways past the historical backdrop of this country and its occupants. Happy deer hunting or chasing!

THE END